Bible Atlas
A first reference book

By Etta Wilson and Sally Lloyd Jones
Illustrated by Steven D. Schindler

STANDARD
PUBLISHING

Abraham leaves home

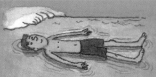

Abraham packs his things
Abraham lived in the city of Ur. One day, God said, "Leave your home, your town and all your friends, and go to a special land I'll show you."

So Abraham packed his things and traveled north with his wife, Sarah, and his nephew, Lot. They stopped in Haran for several years.

The special land
At last they came to Canaan. It was beautiful; full of green hills and flowing rivers. "This is your special land," God told Abraham.

So, at a place called Bethel, Abraham and Sarah and Lot unpacked all their things.

When there wasn't enough food in Canaan, Abraham, Sarah and Lot traveled to Egypt to find food. Then they returned to Canaan.

Abraham and Lot say goodbye
Lot and Abraham both had so many sheep and cattle and helpers that there wasn't enough room for them all to live together happily. So they decided to split up.

Lot chose the best looking land. He went east along the Dead Sea to Sodom and Gomorrah. Abraham went to a place called Hebron.

Clothes

People wore long, loose robes woven from sheep's wool.

Homes

I need more goat hair to finish this.

Come here, you!

People lived in tents woven from goats' hair.

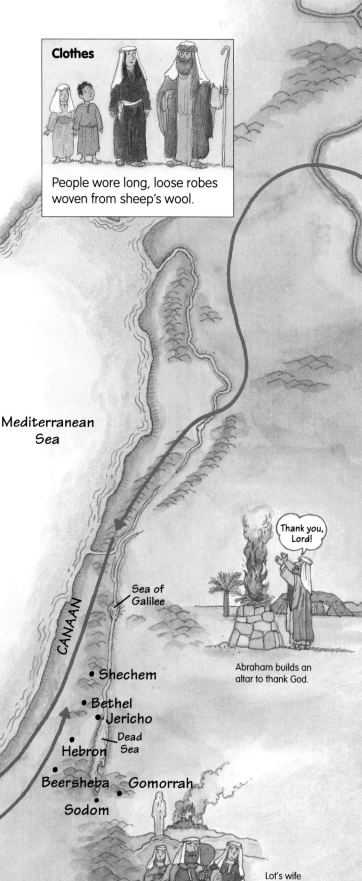

Mediterranean Sea

Thank you, Lord!

Sea of Galilee

CANAAN

• Shechem

• Bethel
• Jericho
Dead Sea

Hebron•

• Beersheba   • Gomorrah

• Sodom

Abraham builds an altar to thank God.

Lot's wife turns to salt.

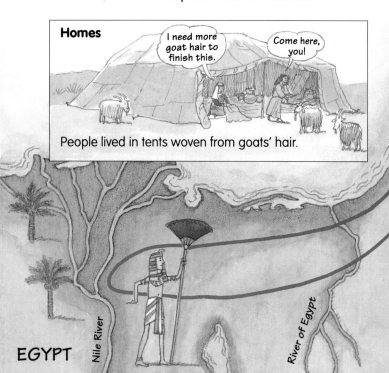

EGYPT

Nile River

River of Egypt

The Nile River is one of the longest in the world: 4,145 miles long!

I don't feel a day over 100!

Abraham lived to be 175 years old! And Sarah was 127 when she died!

EUROPE
Black Sea
Hittites
MESOPOTAMIA
Canaan
EGYPT
Red Sea

Animals

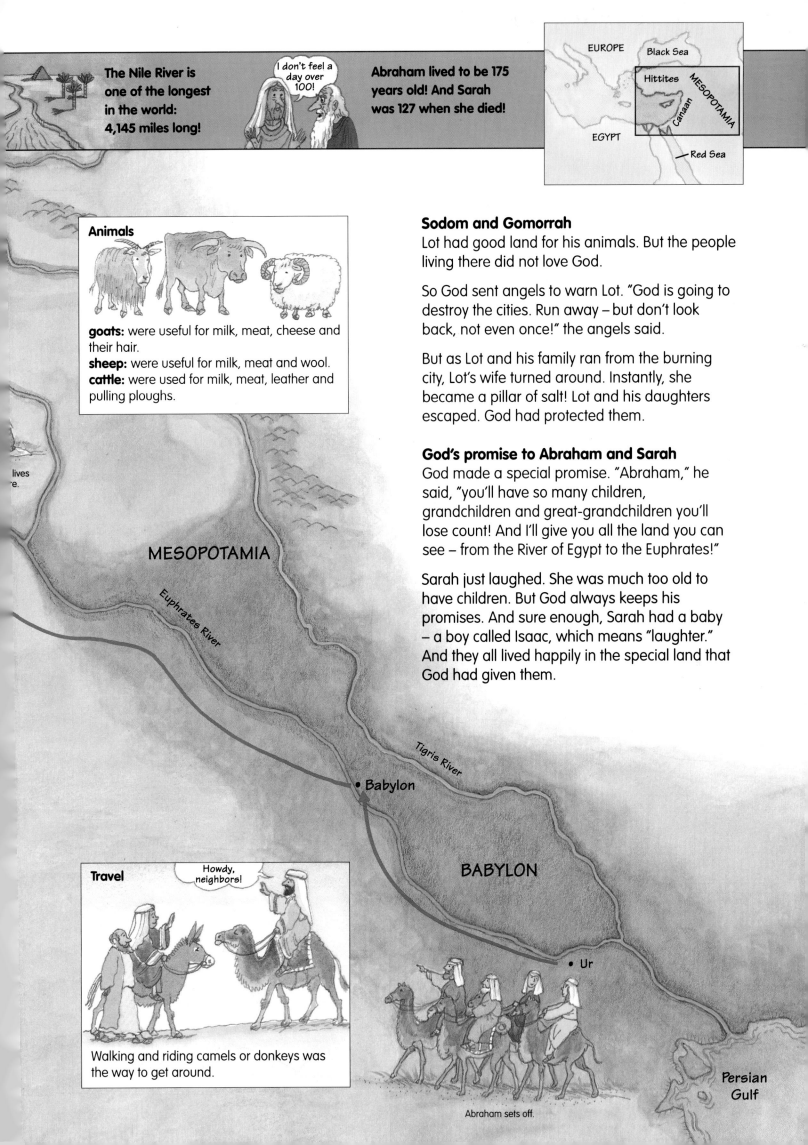

goats: were useful for milk, meat, cheese and their hair.
sheep: were useful for milk, meat and wool.
cattle: were used for milk, meat, leather and pulling ploughs.

lives
e.

MESOPOTAMIA

Euphrates River

Sodom and Gomorrah

Lot had good land for his animals. But the people living there did not love God.

So God sent angels to warn Lot. "God is going to destroy the cities. Run away – but don't look back, not even once!" the angels said.

But as Lot and his family ran from the burning city, Lot's wife turned around. Instantly, she became a pillar of salt! Lot and his daughters escaped. God had protected them.

God's promise to Abraham and Sarah

God made a special promise. "Abraham," he said, "you'll have so many children, grandchildren and great-grandchildren you'll lose count! And I'll give you all the land you can see – from the River of Egypt to the Euphrates!"

Sarah just laughed. She was much too old to have children. But God always keeps his promises. And sure enough, Sarah had a baby – a boy called Isaac, which means "laughter." And they all lived happily in the special land that God had given them.

Tigris River

• Babylon

Travel

Howdy, neighbors!

BABYLON

• Ur

Walking and riding camels or donkeys was the way to get around.

Persian Gulf

Abraham sets off.

Moses and the escape from Egypt

Ooh!

Moses' name means "taken out of the water"!

Better dead than red!

Egyptians neve wore red. They thought it was unlucky!

Living in Egypt

Abraham's grandson, Jacob, ended up living in Egypt with his favorite son, Joseph. Abraham's descendants lived in Egypt for a total of 430 years! They became known as the Israelites, after Jacob, whose name was also Israel.

Rescued by a princess

Pharaoh, the king of Egypt, didn't like the Israelites and made them his slaves. Pharaoh even ordered the Israelites to throw all their baby boys into the Nile River.

But Moses' mother thought of a clever way to save her baby. She put Moses in a basket and hid him in the reeds along the Nile River. Pharaoh's daughter found baby Moses, took him home and cared for him. So Moses grew up like an Egyptian prince!

Moses in hiding

When Moses grew up, he didn't like the way the Egyptians treated the Israelites. He got so angry one day that he killed an Egyptian for beating an Israelite. After this, Moses had to hide in the desert for years.

One day, on Mount Sinai, God spoke to Moses from a bush that was on fire—but didn't burn up! God told Moses to go back to Egypt. God had chosen him to lead the Israelites out of Egypt to God's special land—the Promised Land.

Slaves

Do I hate bricks!

The Israelites had to make bricks for the Egyptians out of mud and straw.

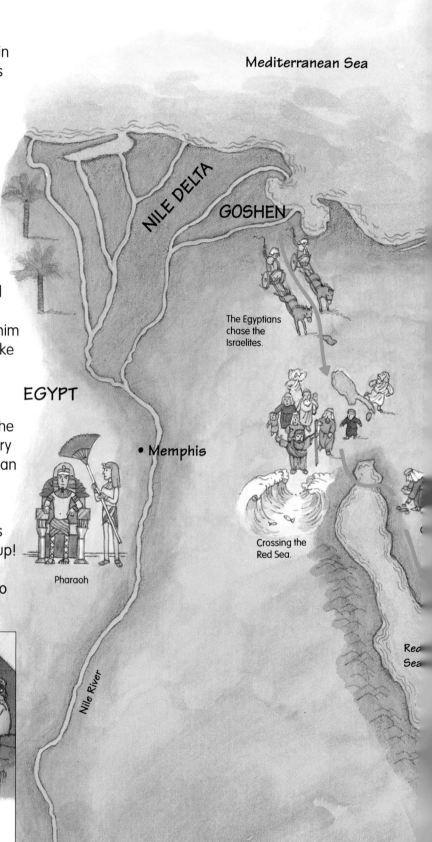

Mediterranean Sea

NILE DELTA

GOSHEN

The Egyptians chase the Israelites.

EGYPT

• Memphis

Pharaoh

Crossing the Red Sea.

Nile River

Rec Sea

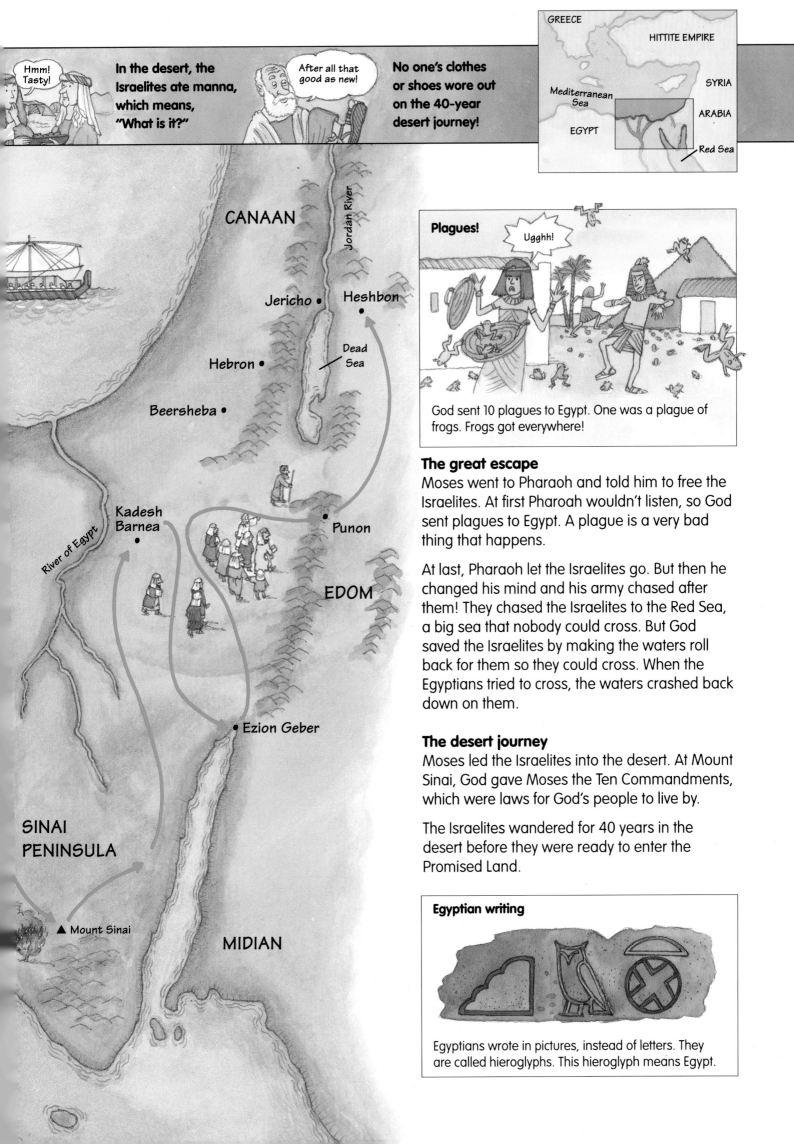

Hmm! Tasty!

In the desert, the Israelites ate manna, which means, "What is it?"

After all that good as new!

No one's clothes or shoes wore out on the 40-year desert journey!

GREECE
HITTITE EMPIRE
SYRIA
Mediterranean Sea
ARABIA
EGYPT
Red Sea

CANAAN

Jordan River

Jericho • • Heshbon

Dead Sea

Hebron •

Beersheba •

Kadesh Barnea •

River of Egypt

• Punon

EDOM

• Ezion Geber

SINAI PENINSULA

▲ Mount Sinai

MIDIAN

Plagues!

Ugghh!

God sent 10 plagues to Egypt. One was a plague of frogs. Frogs got everywhere!

The great escape

Moses went to Pharaoh and told him to free the Israelites. At first Pharoah wouldn't listen, so God sent plagues to Egypt. A plague is a very bad thing that happens.

At last, Pharaoh let the Israelites go. But then he changed his mind and his army chased after them! They chased the Israelites to the Red Sea, a big sea that nobody could cross. But God saved the Israelites by making the waters roll back for them so they could cross. When the Egyptians tried to cross, the waters crashed back down on them.

The desert journey

Moses led the Israelites into the desert. At Mount Sinai, God gave Moses the Ten Commandments, which were laws for God's people to live by.

The Israelites wandered for 40 years in the desert before they were ready to enter the Promised Land.

Egyptian writing

Egyptians wrote in pictures, instead of letters. They are called hieroglyphs. This hieroglyph means Egypt.

Joshua and the Promised Land

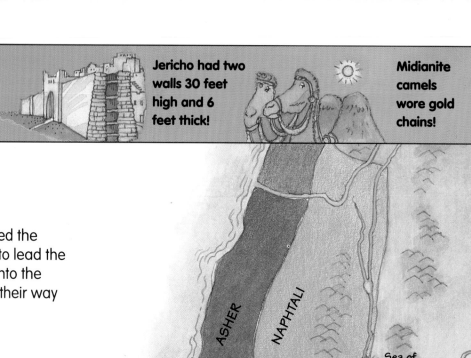

A new leader

Moses died before the Israelites reached the Promised Land. So God chose Joshua to lead the Israelites across the Jordan River and into the Promised Land. But one thing stood in their way – the walled city of Jericho.

Spies in Jericho!

Joshua sent two spies into Jericho to find out what the city was like. The spies stayed at the house of a woman called Rahab.

The king of Jericho heard about the spies. He told Rahab to hand over the spies, but she hid them on her roof. Rahab knew that God was with the Israelites and that she should help them. So she told the king that the spies had already left the city.

While the king's men were off looking for the spies, Rahab helped the spies escape. The spies promised her she would be safe when they captured Jericho.

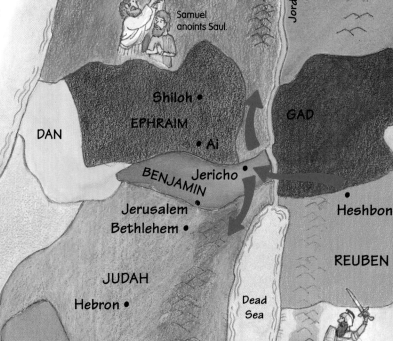

ASHER

NAPHTALI

Sea of Galilee

ZEBULUN

ISSACHAR

MANASSEH

MANA

Jordan River

Samuel anoints Saul.

Shiloh •

EPHRAIM

DAN

• Ai

GAD

BENJAMIN

Jericho •

Jerusalem •

Heshbon

Bethlehem •

Mediterranean Sea

REUBEN

JUDAH

Philistines

Hebron •

Dead Sea

• Beersheba

SIMEON

Moabites

Edomites

 Gideon was a judge of Israel; and he had 70 sons!

 Forget donkeys- God has plans for you!

When Samuel met Saul, Saul was out chasing lost donkeys!

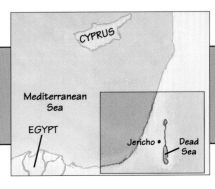

A narrow escape

Easy does it!

Rahab lowered the two spies out of the city through her window using a rope!

The ark of the covenant

The ark of the covenant was a special gold box. It held the two stone tablets of the Ten Commandments, and other reminders of the Israelites' journey to the Promised Land.

Neighbors

The Canaanites were all the people living in the Promised Land when the Israelites entered it. The Canaanites worshiped many false gods.

The walls fall down!

God gave Joshua special instructions on how to capture Jericho. The priests walked in a circle around Jericho for six days carrying the ark of the covenant. On the seventh day, they circled the city seven times and blew their trumpets. Then all the people shouted, and the walls of the city just fell down! The battle was won!

The twelve tribes

When the Israelites entered the Promised Land, Joshua divided up the land between the 12 tribes of Israel.

We want a king!

After Joshua died, the people were ruled by special leaders called Judges. But some years later the Israelites decided they needed a king to help them fight their enemies. God told them them that he was their king. But they wanted a man. So God told the last Judge, Samuel, to choose Saul as king of Israel.

A clever trick!

Whoa! That's moldy! I guess you have come quite a distance. Put her here!

Glad to know ya!

When a tribe called the Gibeonites heard about the capture of Jericho, they were afraid. So they pretended they didn't live in Canaan at all and that they were just travelers. They put on rags and packed moldy bread to pretend they'd traveled for a long time! The trick worked! Joshua made peace with them!

A time of heroes

David and Goliath
King Saul fought many battles with the Philistines. Once, the Philistines sent their giant, Goliath, to dare anyone to fight him. David was just a boy but he killed Goliath with only a sling and one small stone.

Everyone loved David. But Saul was jealous and tried to kill David, so David ran away to hide. After Saul died, David became king. David wrote many psalms and he ruled wisely.

King Solomon – the wisest king
David had a son named Solomon. God made Solomon very wise and people came miles to ask him hard questions. Solomon was rich and built a temple in Jerusalem to thank God.

God's people split up
After Solomon died, the 12 tribes of Israel split into two countries. The 10 tribes in the north were called Israel and the two in the south were called Judah. The kings of Israel did not love God. They taught God's people to worship idols. So did some of Judah's kings. God sent prophets to both Israel and Judah to tell them how to live.

King Ahab and Elijah's dare
King Ahab of Israel made God angry by getting people to worship Baal, a false Canaanite god. So God sent the prophet Elijah to dare Ahab to prove Baal was real. They both built altars and called on their god to light them. Nothing happened to Baal's altar, but Elijah's altar blazed with fire!

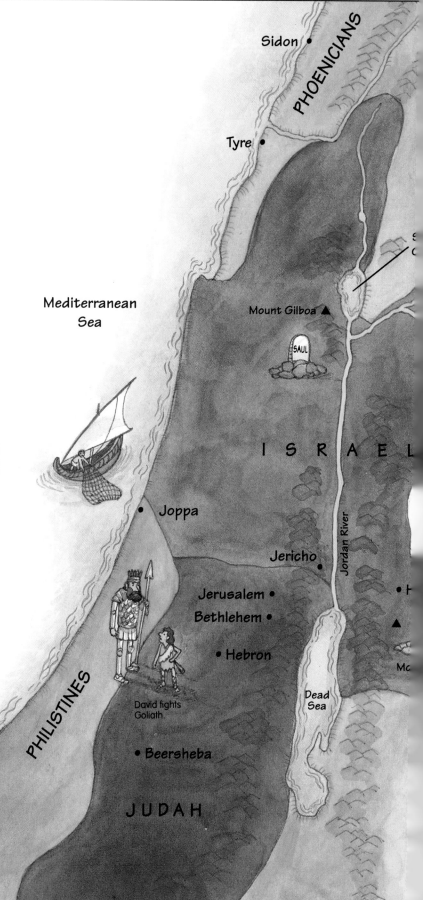

PHOENICIANS

Sidon

Tyre

Mediterranean Sea

Mount Gilboa ▲

SAUL

I S R A E L

Joppa

Jordan River

Jericho

Jerusalem

Bethlehem

Hebron

Dead Sea

PHILISTINES

David fights Goliath.

Beersheba

J U D A H

EGYPT

346.

You're 634, or 436?

King Solomon had 700 wives!

Boy this is heavy!

Naaman took home dirt from Israel to worship God on the same ground!

ASIA MINOR   ASSYRIA
Nineveh •
Mediterranean Sea
Babylon •
Jerusalem •

Trading

Solomon traded copper from his mines for goods from other countries. Solomon imported 40,000 horses into Israel! He used ships built by Phoenicians.

Clothes

Nice threads!

Oh yes, Sire, the finest silk... I can get it for you wholesale!

Solomon dressed in silks from Egypt, Mesopotamia, Africa and India! His robes even had jewels in them!

Daniel

So, this is your den. Nice space!

The Babylonians captured Daniel and took him to Babylon. Daniel wouldn't stop praying to God so he was thrown to the lions. But God kept Daniel safe!

The Prophet Elisha

After Elijah died, Elisha became a prophet. A man named Naaman had leprosy, a bad skin disease. Elisha told Naaman to wash in the Jordan River and Naaman was healed!

King Hezekiah

The people of Israel kept on worshiping idols, so God let the Assyrians defeat them and take them captive. But Judah had a good king called Hezekiah. He prayed and God protected Judah.

Jeremiah

In time, the people of Judah forgot about God. So God sent Jeremiah to warn them, but they would not listen. Then the Babylonians invaded Judah and took the people captive.

Ezra and Nehemiah

After 70 years in captivity, God allowed his people to return to Judah. Ezra and Nehemiah were great leaders who made sure the people worshiped God.

Jonah

Heave Ho!

God sent Jonah from Joppa to warn his enemies in Nineveh that God would punish them. Jonah ran away and ended up in deep water! But God sent a big fish to save him! And God spared Nineveh.

Jesus is born

Journey to Bethlehem

Israel was now part of the Roman Empire. The Roman ruler wanted to count how many people he ruled over. He ordered everyone to go to their home town to be counted.

Mary and Joseph had to travel all the way back to Bethlehem to be counted. Mary was pregnant. When they arrived, Bethlehem was so crowded that the only place they could find to stay was in a stable. And that's where Jesus was born.

The shepherds

On the hills outside Bethlehem, shepherds watched their sheep. Suddenly an angel appeared and told them a king had been born. They hurried to Bethlehem and worshiped Jesus.

A special visit

Meanwhile, some wise men from the East had seen a special star. They knew a new king had been born. They traveled to Jerusalem to ask King Herod if he knew where the new king was.

King Herod didn't like the sound of a new king. Herod told them to let him know when they found Jesus. Secretly, Herod wanted to kill Jesus.

The wise men followed the star to Bethlehem, where they found Jesus, who was now about one year old. They gave Jesus gifts. The wise men realized Herod was bad, so they did not tell him where Jesus was before they went home.

The Roman Empire

Herod, you've certainly got your work cut out for you!

The Roman Empire was so large that the emperor couldn't rule over it all by himself. So he appointed rulers to govern over different parts of the empire. King Herod was a Jewish ruler, appointed by the emperor, Caesar Augustus.

Gold, frankincense and myrrh

Gold! Frankincense! Myrrh!

The wise men's gifts predicted the future! Gold showed Jesus would be a king; frankincense showed he would be a priest; myrrh showed his death would be special.

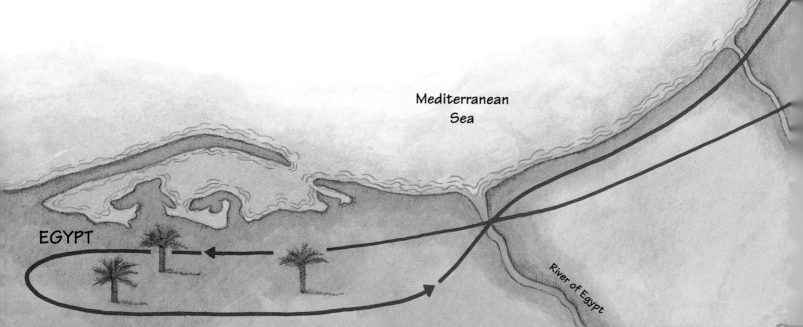

Mediterranean Sea

EGYPT

River of Egypt

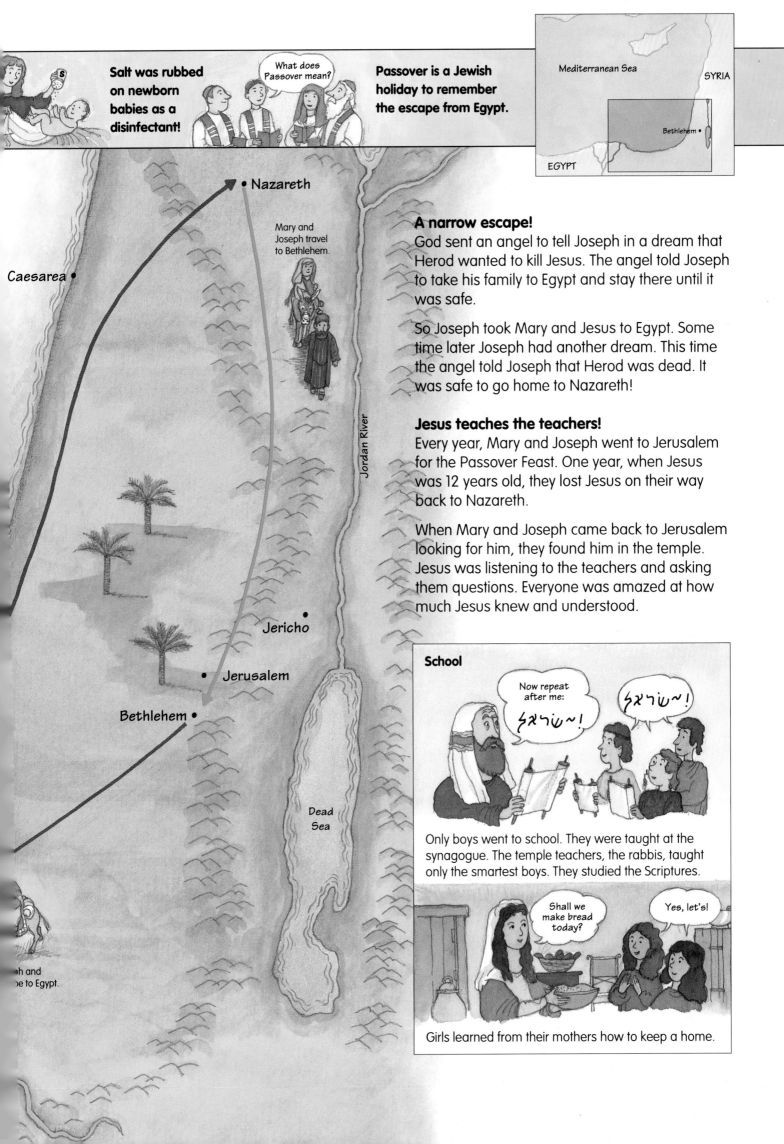

Salt was rubbed on newborn babies as a disinfectant!

What does Passover mean?

Passover is a Jewish holiday to remember the escape from Egypt.

Mediterranean Sea

SYRIA

Bethlehem •

EGYPT

Nazareth

Mary and Joseph travel to Bethlehem.

Caesarea •

Jordan River

Jericho

Jerusalem

Bethlehem •

Dead Sea

h and e to Egypt.

A narrow escape!

God sent an angel to tell Joseph in a dream that Herod wanted to kill Jesus. The angel told Joseph to take his family to Egypt and stay there until it was safe.

So Joseph took Mary and Jesus to Egypt. Some time later Joseph had another dream. This time the angel told Joseph that Herod was dead. It was safe to go home to Nazareth!

Jesus teaches the teachers!

Every year, Mary and Joseph went to Jerusalem for the Passover Feast. One year, when Jesus was 12 years old, they lost Jesus on their way back to Nazareth.

When Mary and Joseph came back to Jerusalem looking for him, they found him in the temple. Jesus was listening to the teachers and asking them questions. Everyone was amazed at how much Jesus knew and understood.

School

Now repeat after me:

Only boys went to school. They were taught at the synagogue. The temple teachers, the rabbis, taught only the smartest boys. They studied the Scriptures.

Shall we make bread today?

Yes, let's!

Girls learned from their mothers how to keep a home.

Jesus' work begins

These are good honey-dipped!

John the Baptist wore camel skins and ate wild honey and locusts!

What's he doing?

When Jesus healed a blind man, he used mud!

Jesus is baptized

When Jesus was grown up, John the Baptist baptized him in the Jordan River. Then Jesus went into the desert for 40 days to prepare for his new work.

Jesus left Nazareth and traveled around Galilee preaching. Jesus spent most of the time teaching and healing people in Galilee.

Fishers of men

One day, by the Sea of Galilee, Jesus called out to some fishermen, "Come and follow me and I'll teach you how to catch men for God!" The fishermen dropped their nets and followed Jesus. As he traveled, Jesus gathered many followers, or disciples.

Miracle at a wedding

One time, Jesus, his disciples and Jesus' mother, Mary, were at a wedding in Cana. Suddenly the wine ran out, so Jesus turned some water into wine! This was his first miracle. A miracle is something special only God can do.

Weddings

Have we been here two days?

At least!

Jewish weddings could last a few days! People played music and had a big feast with lots of bread and fruit and cheese.

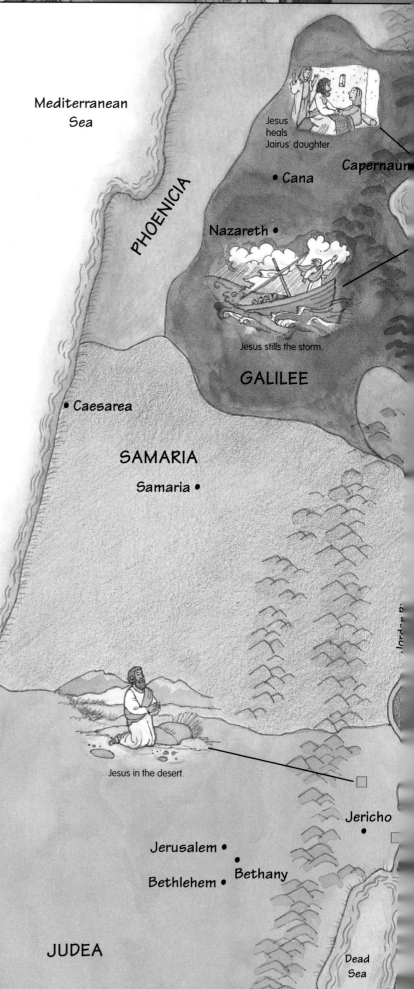

Mediterranean Sea

PHOENICIA

Jesus heals Jairus' daughter.

• Cana

Capernaum

Nazareth •

Jesus stills the storm.

GALILEE

• Caesarea

SAMARIA

Samaria •

Jesus in the desert.

Jericho
•

Jerusalem •
• Bethany
Bethlehem •

JUDEA

Dead Sea

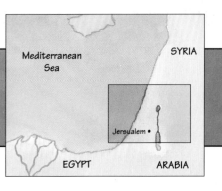

noa!

Peter caught a fish with a coin in its mouth!

The Sea of Galilee was dangerous; storms came without warning!

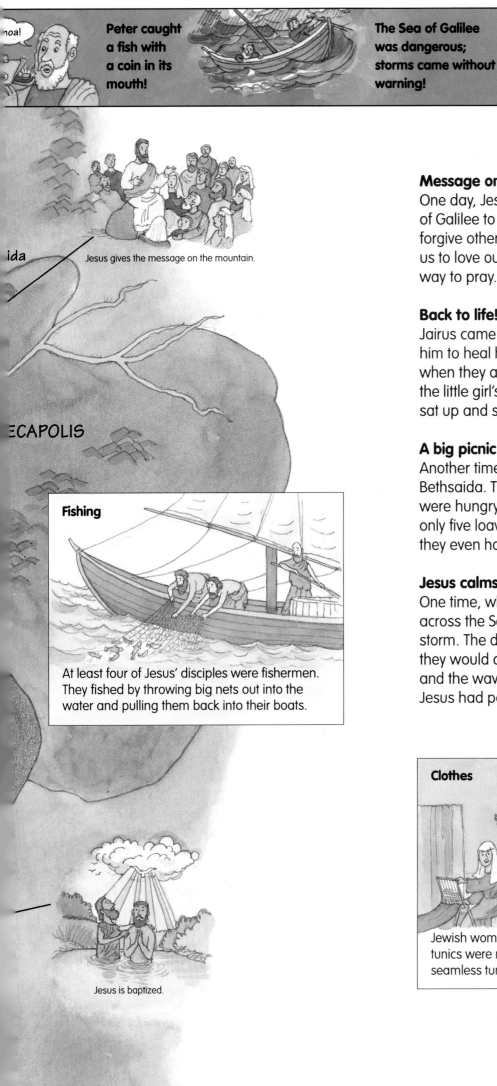

Jesus gives the message on the mountain.

ida

ECAPOLIS

Fishing

At least four of Jesus' disciples were fishermen. They fished by throwing big nets out into the water and pulling them back into their boats.

Jesus is baptized.

Message on a mountain

One day, Jesus went up a mountain by the Sea of Galilee to preach. He taught that we should forgive others just as God forgives us. He taught us to love our enemies and he taught us a new way to pray. It is called the Lord's Prayer.

Back to life!

Jairus came to Jesus in Capernaum and begged him to heal his little girl. Jesus went with him but when they arrived the child was dead. Jesus held the little girl's hand and told her to get up. She sat up and smiled. She was alive again!

A big picnic

Another time, Jesus was preaching near Bethsaida. Thousands of people came and they were hungry. Jesus fed them – all of them – with only five loaves of bread and two small fish! And they even had leftovers!

Jesus calms a storm

One time, when Jesus and his disciples sailed across the Sea of Galilee, there was a fierce storm. The disciples were frightened and thought they would drown. But Jesus spoke to the wind and the waves. "Be still!" he said. And they were! Jesus had power over even the wind and waves!

Clothes

Jewish women wove long shirts called tunics. These tunics were made all in one piece. Jesus wore a seamless tunic.

Jesus in Jerusalem

A hero's welcome
Jesus rode a donkey from Bethany into Jerusalem. People waved palm branches and laid their coats in his path. They shouted with joy, "Hosanna in the Highest!"

A den of thieves!
Jesus went into the Jerusalem temple. But he found it full of money-changers and merchants cheating people. He pushed over their tables and turned them out of God's house.

A special meal
Later that week, Jesus ate the Passover meal in the upper room with his disciples. Jesus blessed the bread and the cup before he gave it to them. He told them to do this to remember him.

Betrayed by a friend
After dinner, Jesus and his disciples went to the Garden of Gethsemane, on the Mount of Olives, to pray. Judas, one of Jesus' friends, led a group of soldiers to the garden to arrest Jesus.

Upper room

Have you seen Peter anywhere?

He's just behind us!

The Passover Feast was held in an upper room. An upper room was a small room built in one corner of the roof of a house.

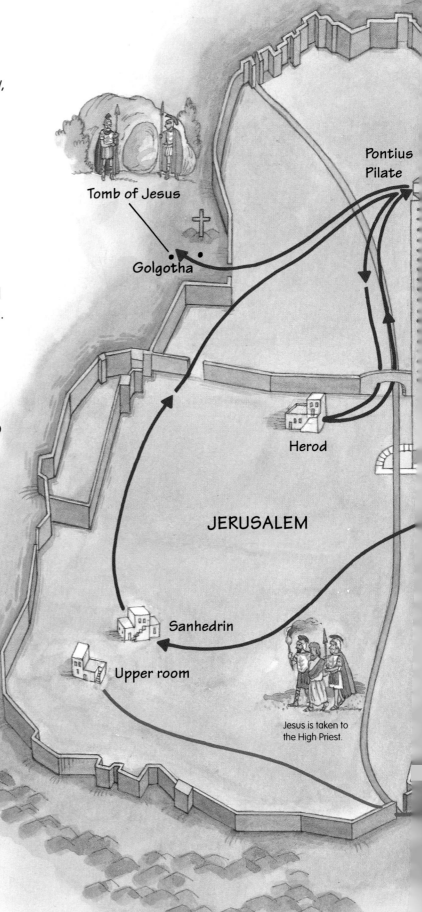

Tomb of Jesus

Golgotha

Pontius Pilate

Herod

JERUSALEM

Sanhedrin

Upper room

Jesus is taken to the High Priest.

Golgotha means, "the place of the skull."

Jesus cooked his disciples breakfast on the beach soon after he rose again!

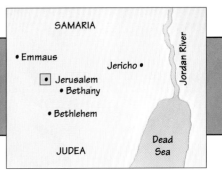

SAMARIA
• Emmaus
Jericho •
☐ Jerusalem
• Bethany
• Bethlehem
JUDEA
Jordan River
Dead Sea

Pool of Bethesda

Sanhedrin

The Sanhedrin was the Jewish high court. It had 71 members: priests, lawyers, and elders. They met in the house of Caiaphas, the High Priest.

Mount of Olives ▲

Jesus enters Jerusalem from Bethany.

Garden of Gethsemane

Jesus and the disciples go to Gethsemane.

The greatest sacrifice

The soldiers took Jesus to the Sanhedrin. The Jewish leaders wanted to get rid of Jesus because he said he was God's Son. They put Jesus on trial and found him guilty and sent him to Pontius Pilate, the Roman governor.

Pilate sent Jesus to Herod. But Herod didn't want to make a decision about Jesus, so he sent him back to Pilate. The Jewish leaders convinced Pilate to order Jesus' death. Jesus carried his cross to Golgotha, where he was crucified. He was buried in a tomb carved out from rock and a large stone was placed in front of the entrance.

He is risen!

A few days later, when Mary Magdalene came to anoint Jesus' body with spices, she found the stone rolled away and the tomb empty. An angel said to Mary, "Jesus is alive!"

Mary told the disciples, but they didn't believe her until Jesus came to see them himself.

Jesus goes to Heaven

Jesus stayed with the disciples for a month. Then he took them up to a mountain outside Jerusalem. They watched as Jesus went back to Heaven.

Money changers

According to this, you are owed five temple coins for your Roman coin.

Foreign coins had pictures of people on them. The Jews said these were "graven images" so they were not allowed into the temple. Visitors had to swap them for Jewish coins. Money changers did this job and they often cheated.

Peter spreads the word!

Bwana Asifiwe! 子そ!

At Pentecost, the disciples spoke in languages they'd never learned!

Not Rocky. Just Rock. OK?

Jesus ga Peter a nicknam was "roc

Pentecost

After Jesus went home to Heaven, the disciples stayed in Jerusalem. On the day of Pentecost Jesus sent them his special helper, the Holy Spirit. After that, they could preach boldly and many people believed in Jesus.

A lame man walks!

One day, two of Jesus' disciples, Peter and John, went to the temple. They saw a crippled man begging for money. Peter said to the man, "I don't have money, but what I have I give you. In the name of Jesus Christ of Nazareth, walk!" The man jumped to his feet and walked!

The disciples in prison

Meanwhile, the Jewish leaders were unhappy. They thought people would start following Jesus. They ordered Peter and John to stop preaching. But they wouldn't. So they put the disciples in prison. But not for long – that night God's angel set them free!

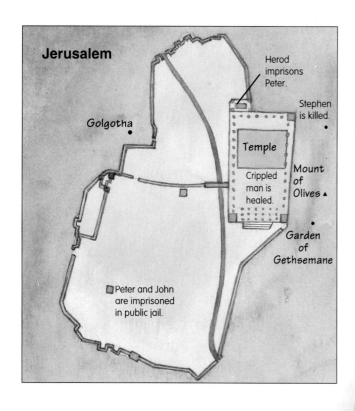

Jerusalem

Golgotha

Herod imprisons Peter.

Stephen is killed.

Temple

Crippled man is healed.

Mount of Olives ▲

Garden of Gethsemane

Peter and John are imprisoned in public jail.

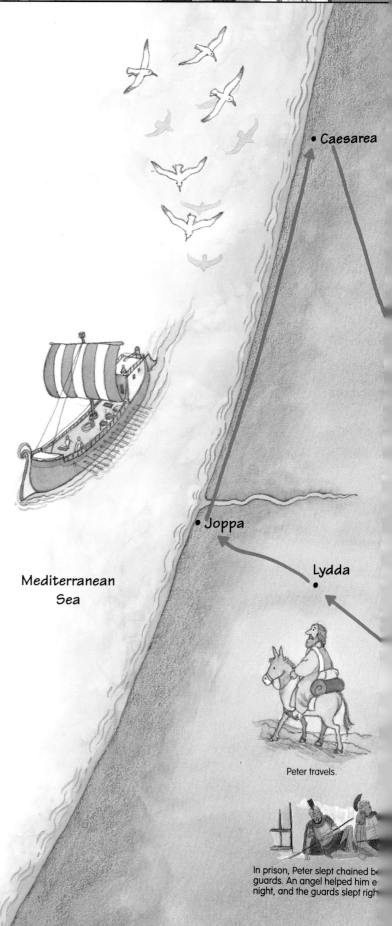

• Caesarea

• Joppa

Lydda •

Mediterranean Sea

Peter travels.

In prison, Peter slept chained be guards. An angel helped him e night, and the guards slept righ

Believers used a secret sign so Christians would know them; a fish!

They're calling us Christians.

Hmm! Sounds fine.

Believers were first called Christians at Antioch!

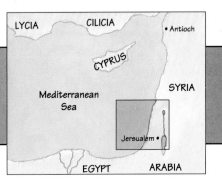

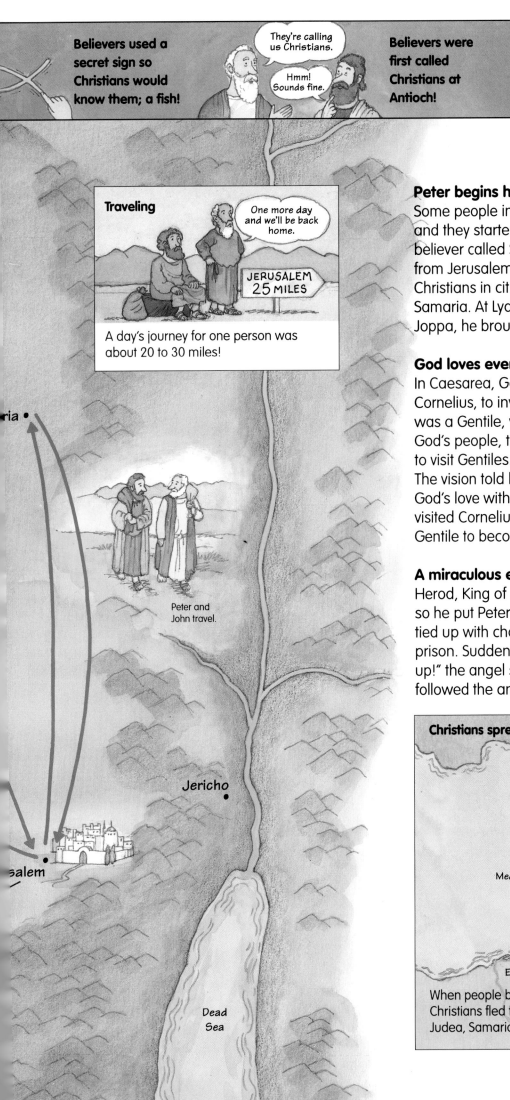

Traveling

One more day and we'll be back home.

JERUSALEM 25 MILES

A day's journey for one person was about 20 to 30 miles!

Peter and John travel.

Jericho

Dead Sea

...ria •

...salem •

Peter begins his travels

Some people in Jerusalem didn't like Christians and they started hurting them. They even killed a believer called Stephen. So some Christians fled from Jerusalem. Peter went to preach to these Christians in cities throughout Judea and Samaria. At Lydda, he healed a crippled man. In Joppa, he brought Tabitha back to life!

God loves everyone!

In Caesarea, God told a Roman centurion, Cornelius, to invite Peter to visit him. Cornelius was a Gentile, which means he was not part of God's people, the Jews. Jews were not supposed to visit Gentiles. Meanwhile, Peter had a vision. The vision told him that Jesus had come to share God's love with everyone, even Gentiles. Peter visited Cornelius and Cornelius was the first Gentile to become a Christian!

A miraculous escape!

Herod, King of Judea, didn't like Peter preaching, so he put Peter in prison. One night, Peter was tied up with chains between two soldiers in prison. Suddenly, an angel appeared. "Quick, get up!" the angel said. Peter's chains fell off and he followed the angel out of prison!

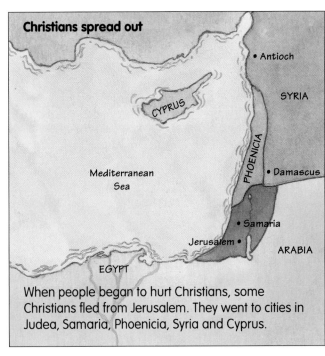

Christians spread out

When people began to hurt Christians, some Christians fled from Jerusalem. They went to cities in Judea, Samaria, Phoenicia, Syria and Cyprus.

Paul's journeys

Paul spent a whole day and night floating at sea!

Paul told the Corinthi[ans] following Jesus is like running a race; Corin[th] loved athletics!

Saul makes a change

Saul was a Jew who didn't like Christians and tried to get rid of them. One day, Saul went to Damascus looking for Christians. On the way, a bright light struck Saul down and Jesus spoke to him. When Saul opened his eyes, he was blind!

For three days Saul couldn't see. God sent a Christian, Ananias, to heal him. When Saul could see again, he became a Christian. He changed his ways, and, later, his name – to Paul!

Paul sets sail

Paul traveled around, spreading the good news about Jesus. On his first long trip, he took his friend, Barnabas. At Lystra, Paul healed a crippled man. People thought they were gods because they did miracles. Paul's first trip took two years!

Paul's adventures

On Paul's second trip, Silas, Timothy and Luke traveled with him. They traveled through Macedonia and Greece. In Macedonia, they baptized Lydia and healed a servant girl. Paul and Silas were thrown in prison in Philippi.

That night God sent an earthquake, the prison doors flew open and their chains fell off! Paul and Silas didn't run away. Instead, they told the jailer and his family about Jesus. They became Christians and Paul and Silas were freed.

On his third trip, Paul went to Ephesus for three years. On his way back to Jerusalem he visited Macedonia and Greece.

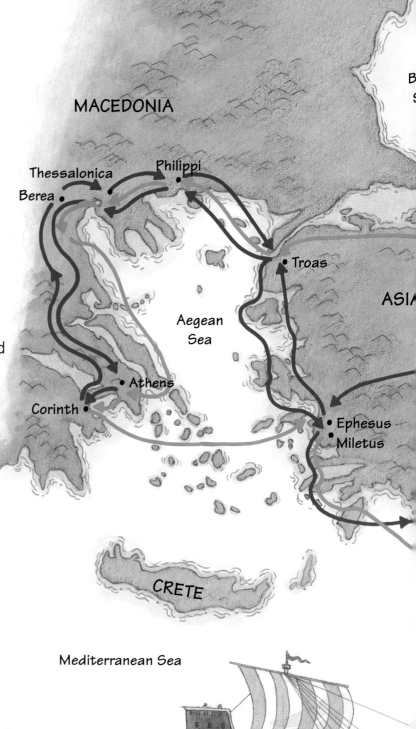

MACEDONIA

Thessalonica
Berea
Philippi
Troas
ASIA
Aegean Sea
Athens
Corinth
Ephesus
Miletus
CRETE
Mediterranean Sea

Letters

That's it for this morning... let's write the Ephesians after lunch...

Many books in the New Testament are actually letters. Paul had different friends who wrote his letters for him.

⟶ Paul's first journey

⟶ Paul's second journey

⟶ Paul's third journey

Better ship it bulk rate!

Paul's longest letter is the book of Romans!

Yow!

Paul was bitten by a viper but he didn't die; God kept him safe!

Paul's journey to Rome

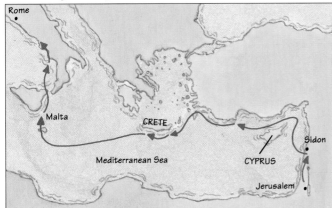

Paul goes to Rome

When Paul went back to Jerusalem, he was arrested and sent to Rome for trial. On the way to Rome, Paul was shipwrecked on Malta. While he was there, Paul healed people and preached.

In Rome, Paul was kept under guard, but he kept on preaching – even to his Roman guards! In prison, Paul wrote to churches he had visited. Some of these letters are in the New Testament.

Christians everywhere!

The Romans tried to get rid of Christians. But Christians conquered Rome; not with swords and fighting but with love and faith!

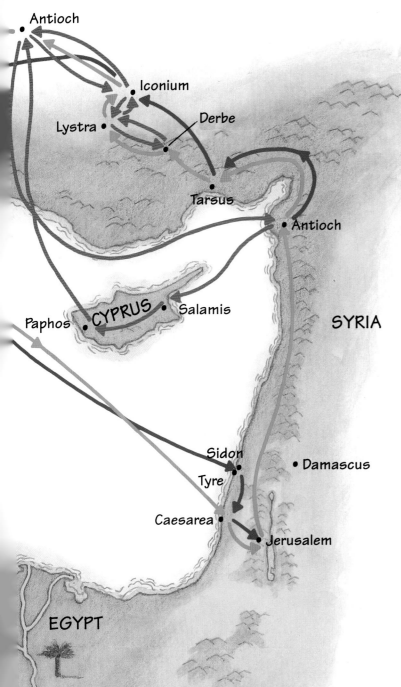

Christians today

Today, there are Christians in places Peter and Paul had never even heard of! Christians make up about two-sevenths of the world's population. That's a lot of people in a lot of countries!